MW01502502

Get Your Stuff **Done!**

The Easy-to-Use Journal and Project Planner That
Will Help You Finish What You Start

IZOLDA TRAKHTENBERG

DEDICATION

To all of you who've tried everything and keep trying anyway.

CONTENTS

ACKNOWLEDGMENTS

Nothing is achieved without help. I'm grateful to so many who played a role in shaping this journal. Their insights and ideas shaped much of you'll use.

I also give thanks to Alec, Carol, Farah, and Todd for their participation in the mastermind that finalized the *Get Your Stuff Done* program. They went through the mastermind to work through the kinks and streamline the process. I also thank Eric, Barbara, Julia, Mike, Patty, Kirstin, Lauren, Ann, Marcia, Brecken, Jane, and Virginia for evaluating the original version of this journal. They helped make it what it is today.

I send gratitude to my sisters Emily, Golda, and my sister from another mister, Kristen. Without your love and support, I'd be lost. With your love and support, I soar.

I'm always grateful to my husband Rich and our kitties Kimba and Ninja for putting up with my ramblings. They supported me as I developed this simple and effective system of organizing your thoughts, capturing your ideas, and developing a process for getting stuff done.

1 HOW TO USE THIS JOURNAL

If you've been tearing your hair out trying to get everything done, you're in the right place. We're overworked and hyper-stimulated. We have so much coming at us it's a wonder we get anything done. The productivity systems I tried had too many bells and whistles. I needed something simple. So, I developed this journal. It's easy to use, and it will help you get your stuff done. No muss. No fuss.

Here's how to use it. **First**, put the journal by your bedside. Tonight, when you get in bed, fill out page **3**. If this is your first journal, number it *1*. This is how you'll track your progress as you dive into your unique method of productivity and achievement.

Next, write down your personal and professional visions for these next three months. What do you want to achieve? What will it look like when you succeed in realizing both?

Then, imagine your reward for achieving your goals. Some people think finishing is sufficient reward, but I like to treat myself when I achieve. Usually, I travel, or I buy myself a new musical instrument. How will you reward yourself? Write it down on page **3**. Tomorrow get in bed ten minutes earlier than usual.

Fill out page **4**.

1. *Gratitude*. List three things you're grateful for.
2. *Check-in*. Write how you feel. What did you think of how today went? Get a general sense of where you are. And keep it short and sweet.
3. *Tomorrow, I will*. Focus in and write down your intention for tomorrow. No matter how you did today, tomorrow is another opportunity to stretch, grow, and achieve your goals.

The following morning get up fifteen minutes earlier than usual. Write the free-write. Write about anything that comes into your mind. Don't stop and think. This is a morning brain data dump. If you have a realization, mark it with an asterisk. If you get an idea to follow-up on, use a star. If you think of a to-do-list item, use a hash tag. After you finish, you'll have a ready-made list of things you can include in your check-in, gratitude list, or projects. That evening you'll complete the next page.

1. **Gratitude.** List three things you're grateful for. Each day think of three new things.

2. **Today's Wins.** Write today's victories and other "Yes!" events to keep excited for next steps.

3. **Check-in.** Write how you feel right now. What did you think of how today went? Get a general sense of where you are. And keep it short and sweet.

4. **Tomorrow, I will.** Focus in and write down your intention for tomorrow. No matter how you did today, tomorrow is another opportunity to stretch, grow, and achieve your goals.

5. **Projects.** Write three projects (only three) you want to work on today. For every project, write three tasks to complete. As you complete each task, mark it with in X. Don't do more than three projects or three tasks per project. You might have more than three tasks for one project and that's OK. You can put the same project on twice. Our brains work best when we think in threes. So, stay efficient and productive. Give yourself the best opportunity to get stuff done. The goal is to develop a system that works for your unique architecture. This Project-based process is a great way to start.

Every week

Fill out your key accomplishments, realizations, process, and feelings. Note your concerns and your victories. Keep track so you can keep making progress.

Are you ready? Head to the next page and get started!

Journal Number:

_____

Date:

_____

My Personal Vision for the next three months

_____

_____

_____

_____

My Professional Vision for the next three months

_____

_____

_____

_____

My Reward

At the end of this journal, I encourage you to reward yourself for your hard work. What will that reward be? Write it below.

_____

_____

_____

_____

I'm grateful for

1. _____
2. _____
3. _____

Check-in

_____

_____

_____

Tomorrow, I will

_____

_____

_____

Date   State of Mind

_____

_____

_____

_____

_____

_____

_____

_____

_____

_____

_____

_____

_____

_____

_____

_____

_____

_____

_____

_____

_____

_____

_____

_____

_____

_____

_____

✳ = Realizations   ★ = Ideas   # = To-do Items   Get Your Stuff Done!

I'm grateful for

1. _____

2. _____

3. _____

Today's Action Goals

Project: _____

☐ _____

☐ _____

☐ _____

Project: _____

☐ _____

☐ _____

☐ _____

Project: _____

☐ _____

☐ _____

☐ _____

Today's Wins

_____

_____

_____

Check-in

_____

_____

_____

Tomorrow, I will

_____

_____

_____

Date   State of Mind

✳ = Realizations ★ = Ideas # = To-do Items Get Your Stuff Done!

I'm grateful for

1. _____
2. _____
3. _____

Today's Action Goals

Project: _____
- ☐ _____
- ☐ _____
- ☐ _____

Project: _____
- ☐ _____
- ☐ _____
- ☐ _____

Project: _____
- ☐ _____
- ☐ _____
- ☐ _____

Today's Wins

_____
_____
_____

Check-in

_____
_____
_____

Tomorrow, I will

_____
_____
_____

Date State of Mind

I'm grateful for

1. _____
2. _____
3. _____

Today's Action Goals

Project: _____
- ☐ _____
- ☐ _____
- ☐ _____

Project: _____
- ☐ _____
- ☐ _____
- ☐ _____

Project: _____
- ☐ _____
- ☐ _____
- ☐ _____

Today's Wins

_____
_____
_____

Check-in

_____
_____
_____

Tomorrow, I will

_____
_____
_____

Date   State of Mind

_____

_____

_____

_____

_____

_____

_____

_____

_____

_____

_____

_____

_____

_____

_____

_____

_____

_____

_____

_____

_____

_____

_____

_____

_____

_____

* = Realizations   ★ = Ideas   # = To-do Items   Get Your Stuff Done!

I'm grateful for

1. _____
2. _____
3. _____

Today's Action Goals

Project: _____

☐ _____
☐ _____
☐ _____

Project: _____

☐ _____
☐ _____
☐ _____

Project: _____

☐ _____
☐ _____
☐ _____

Today's Wins

_____
_____
_____

Check-in

_____
_____
_____

Tomorrow, I will

_____
_____
_____

Date   State of Mind

_____

_____

_____

_____

_____

_____

_____

_____

_____

_____

_____

_____

_____

_____

_____

_____

_____

_____

_____

_____

_____

_____

_____

_____

_____

_____

_____

_____

_____

_____

✳ = Realizations   ★ = Ideas   # = To-do Items   Get Your Stuff Done!

I'm grateful for

1. _____

2. _____

3. _____

Today's Action Goals

Project: _____

☐ _____

☐ _____

☐ _____

Project: _____

☐ _____

☐ _____

☐ _____

Project: _____

☐ _____

☐ _____

☐ _____

Today's Wins

_____

_____

_____

Check-in

_____

_____

_____

Tomorrow, I will

_____

_____

_____

Date   State of Mind

I'm grateful for

1. _____
2. _____
3. _____

Today's Action Goals

Project: _____

☐ _____

☐ _____

☐ _____

Project: _____

☐ _____

☐ _____

☐ _____

Project: _____

☐ _____

☐ _____

☐ _____

Today's Wins

_____

_____

_____

Check-in

_____

_____

_____

Tomorrow, I will

_____

_____

_____

Date   State of Mind

_____

_____

_____

_____

_____

_____

_____

_____

_____

_____

_____

_____

_____

_____

_____

_____

_____

_____

_____

_____

_____

_____

_____

_____

_____

_____

_____

_____

✳ = Realizations   ★ = Ideas   # = To do Items   Get Your Stuff Done!

I'm grateful for

1. _____
2. _____
3. _____

Today's Action Goals

Project: _____

☐ _____

☐ _____

☐ _____

Project: _____

☐ _____

☐ _____

☐ _____

Project: _____

☐ _____

☐ _____

☐ _____

Today's Wins

_____

_____

_____

Check-in

_____

_____

_____

Tomorrow, I will

_____

_____

_____

Weekly Assessment

Key Realizations

_____

_____

_____

_____

_____

Key Accomplishments

_____

_____

_____

_____

_____

Projects I Made Progress On

_____

_____

_____

_____

_____

Projects I Want To Work On

_____

_____

_____

_____

_____

✱ = Realizations   ★ = Ideas   # = To-do Items   Get Your Stuff Done!

Notes

_____

_____

_____

_____

_____

_____

_____

_____

_____

_____

_____

_____

I Feel

_____

_____

_____

_____

_____

_____

_____

_____

_____

_____

_____

_____

Date State of Mind

I'm grateful for

1. _____
2. _____
3. _____

Today's Action Goals

Project: _____

☐ _____
☐ _____
☐ _____

Project: _____

☐ _____
☐ _____
☐ _____

Project: _____

☐ _____
☐ _____
☐ _____

Today's Wins

_____
_____
_____

Check-in

_____
_____
_____

Tomorrow, I will

_____
_____
_____

Date   State of Mind

_____
_____
_____
_____
_____
_____
_____
_____
_____
_____
_____
_____
_____
_____
_____
_____
_____
_____
_____
_____
_____
_____
_____
_____
_____
_____
_____
_____
_____

✳ = Realizations   ★ = Ideas   # = To-do Items   Get Your Stuff Done!

I'm grateful for

1. _____
2. _____
3. _____

Today's Action Goals

Project: _____
- ☐ _____
- ☐ _____
- ☐ _____

Project: _____
- ☐ _____
- ☐ _____
- ☐ _____

Project: _____
- ☐ _____
- ☐ _____
- ☐ _____

Today's Wins

_____

_____

_____

Check-in

_____

_____

_____

Tomorrow, I will

_____

_____

_____

Date   State of Mind

_____

_____

_____

_____

_____

_____

_____

_____

_____

_____

_____

_____

_____

_____

_____

_____

_____

_____

_____

_____

_____

_____

_____

_____

_____

_____

_____

_____

_____

_____

✳ = Realizations   ★ = Ideas   # = To-do Items   Get Your Stuff Done!

I'm grateful for

1. _____
2. _____
3. _____

Today's Action Goals

Project: _____

- ☐ _____
- ☐ _____
- ☐ _____

Project: _____

- ☐ _____
- ☐ _____
- ☐ _____

Project: _____

- ☐ _____
- ☐ _____
- ☐ _____

Today's Wins

_____

_____

_____

Check-in

_____

_____

_____

Tomorrow, I will

_____

_____

_____

Date State of Mind

_____

*= Realizations ★= Ideas # = To-do Items Get Your Stuff Done!

I'm grateful for

1. _____
2. _____
3. _____

Today's Action Goals

Project: _____

☐ _____
☐ _____
☐ _____

Project: _____

☐ _____
☐ _____
☐ _____

Project: _____

☐ _____
☐ _____
☐ _____

Today's Wins

_____
_____
_____

Check-in

_____
_____
_____

Tomorrow, I will

_____
_____
_____

Date   State of Mind

_____
_____
_____
_____
_____
_____
_____
_____
_____
_____
_____
_____
_____
_____
_____
_____
_____
_____
_____
_____
_____
_____
_____
_____
_____
_____
_____
_____
_____
_____
_____
_____

✳ = Realizations   ★ = Ideas   # = To-do Items   Get Your Stuff Done!

I'm grateful for

1. _____
2. _____
3. _____

Today's Action Goals

Project: _____

- ☐ _____
- ☐ _____
- ☐ _____

Project: _____

- ☐ _____
- ☐ _____
- ☐ _____

Project: _____

- ☐ _____
- ☐ _____
- ☐ _____

Today's Wins

_____

_____

_____

Check-in

_____

_____

_____

Tomorrow, I will

_____

_____

_____

Date　　　　　　　　State of Mind

_____

_____

_____

_____

_____

_____

_____

_____

_____

_____

_____

_____

_____

_____

_____

_____

_____

_____

_____

_____

_____

_____

_____

_____

_____

_____

_____

_____

_____

_____

_____

_____

_____

_____

_____

✳ = Realizations　　★ = Ideas　# = To-do Items　Get Your Stuff Done!

I'm grateful for

1.
2.
3.

Today's Action Goals

Project:
- ☐
- ☐
- ☐

Project:
- ☐
- ☐
- ☐

Project:
- ☐
- ☐
- ☐

Today's Wins

Check-in

Tomorrow, I will

Date   State of Mind

_____
_____
_____
_____
_____
_____
_____
_____
_____
_____
_____
_____
_____
_____
_____
_____
_____
_____
_____
_____
_____
_____
_____
_____
_____
_____
_____
_____
_____
_____
_____

✳ = Realizations   ★ = Ideas   # = To-do Items   Get Your Stuff Done!

I'm grateful for

1. _____
2. _____
3. _____

Today's Action Goals

Project: _____

☐ _____
☐ _____
☐ _____

Project: _____

☐ _____
☐ _____
☐ _____

Project: _____

☐ _____
☐ _____
☐ _____

Today's Wins

_____
_____
_____

Check-in

_____
_____
_____

Tomorrow, I will

_____
_____
_____

Weekly Assessment

Key Realizations

_____
_____
_____
_____
_____

Key Accomplishments

_____
_____
_____
_____
_____

Projects I Made Progress On

_____
_____
_____
_____
_____

Projects I Want To Work On

_____
_____
_____
_____
_____

✳ = Realizations   ★ = Ideas   # = To-do Items   Get Your Stuff Done!

Notes

_____
_____
_____
_____
_____
_____
_____
_____
_____
_____
_____
_____

I Feel

_____
_____
_____
_____
_____
_____
_____
_____
_____
_____
_____

Date   State of Mind

I'm grateful for

1. _____
2. _____
3. _____

Today's Action Goals

Project: _____
☐ _____
☐ _____
☐ _____

Project: _____
☐ _____
☐ _____
☐ _____

Project: _____
☐ _____
☐ _____
☐ _____

Today's Wins

_____
_____
_____

Check-in

_____
_____
_____

Tomorrow, I will

_____
_____
_____

Date   State of Mind

_____

_____

_____

_____

_____

_____

_____

_____

_____

_____

_____

_____

_____

_____

_____

_____

_____

_____

_____

_____

_____

_____

_____

_____

_____

_____

_____

_____

✳ = Realizations   ★ = Ideas   # = To-do Items   Get Your Stuff Done!

I'm grateful for

1. _____
2. _____
3. _____

Today's Action Goals

Project: _____
- [ ] _____
- [ ] _____
- [ ] _____

Project: _____
- [ ] _____
- [ ] _____
- [ ] _____

Project: _____
- [ ] _____
- [ ] _____
- [ ] _____

Today's Wins

_____

_____

_____

Check-in

_____

_____

_____

Tomorrow, I will

_____

_____

_____

Date   State of Mind

_____

_____

_____

_____

_____

_____

_____

_____

_____

_____

_____

_____

_____

_____

_____

_____

_____

_____

_____

_____

_____

_____

_____

_____

_____

_____

_____

_____

_____

_____

_____

✳ = Realizations   ★ = Ideas   # = To-do Items   Get Your Stuff Done!

I'm grateful for

1. _____
2. _____
3. _____

Today's Action Goals

Project: _____
- ☐ _____
- ☐ _____
- ☐ _____

Project: _____
- ☐ _____
- ☐ _____
- ☐ _____

Project: _____
- ☐ _____
- ☐ _____
- ☐ _____

Today's Wins

_____

_____

_____

Check-in

_____

_____

_____

Tomorrow, I will

_____

_____

_____

Date   State of Mind

‒‒

✳ = Realizations   ★ = Ideas   # = To-do Items   Get Your Stuff Done!

I'm grateful for

1. _____
2. _____
3. _____

Today's Action Goals

Project: _____

- ☐ _____
- ☐ _____
- ☐ _____

Project: _____

- ☐ _____
- ☐ _____
- ☐ _____

Project: _____

- ☐ _____
- ☐ _____
- ☐ _____

Today's Wins

_____

_____

_____

Check-in

_____

_____

_____

Tomorrow, I will

_____

_____

_____

Date   State of Mind

_____
_____
_____
_____
_____
_____
_____
_____
_____
_____
_____
_____
_____
_____
_____
_____
_____
_____
_____
_____
_____
_____
_____
_____
_____
_____
_____
_____
_____
_____
_____
_____
_____
_____

✳ = Realizations   ★ = Ideas   # = To-do Items   Get Your Stuff Done!

I'm grateful for

1. _____
2. _____
3. _____

Today's Action Goals

Project: _____
- [ ] _____
- [ ] _____
- [ ] _____

Project: _____
- [ ] _____
- [ ] _____
- [ ] _____

Project: _____
- [ ] _____
- [ ] _____
- [ ] _____

Today's Wins

_____

_____

_____

Check-in

_____

_____

_____

Tomorrow, I will

_____

_____

_____

Date   State of Mind

✳ = Realizations   ★ = Ideas   # = To-do Items   Get Your Stuff Done!

I'm grateful for

1.

2.

3.

Today's Action Goals

Project:

- ☐
- ☐
- ☐

Project:

- ☐
- ☐
- ☐

Project:

- ☐
- ☐
- ☐

Today's Wins

Check-in

Tomorrow, I will

Date   State of Mind

I'm grateful for

1. _____
2. _____
3. _____

Today's Action Goals

Project: _____

☐ _____
☐ _____
☐ _____

Project: _____

☐ _____
☐ _____
☐ _____

Project: _____

☐ _____
☐ _____
☐ _____

Today's Wins

_____

_____

_____

Check-in

_____

_____

_____

Tomorrow, I will

_____

_____

_____

Weekly Assessment

Key Realizations

_____

_____

_____

_____

_____

Key Accomplishments

_____

_____

_____

_____

_____

Projects I Made Progress On

_____

_____

_____

_____

Projects I Want To Work On

_____

_____

_____

_____

_____

✳ = Realizations   ★ = Ideas # = To-do Items Get Your Stuff Done!

Notes

_____

_____

_____

_____

_____

_____

_____

_____

_____

_____

_____

I Feel

_____

_____

_____

_____

_____

_____

_____

_____

_____

_____

Date   State of Mind

_____

_____

_____

_____

_____

_____

_____

_____

_____

_____

_____

_____

_____

_____

_____

_____

_____

_____

_____

_____

_____

_____

_____

_____

_____

_____

_____

_____

_____

_____

✳= Realizations   **★**= Ideas   # = To-do Items   Get Your Stuff Done!

I'm grateful for

1. _____
2. _____
3. _____

Today's Action Goals

Project: _____
☐ _____
☐ _____
☐ _____

Project: _____
☐ _____
☐ _____
☐ _____

Project: _____
☐ _____
☐ _____
☐ _____

Today's Wins

_____
_____
_____

Check-in

_____
_____
_____

Tomorrow, I will

_____
_____
_____

Date   State of Mind

_____
_____
_____
_____
_____
_____
_____
_____
_____
_____
_____
_____
_____
_____
_____
_____
_____
_____
_____
_____
_____
_____
_____
_____
_____
_____
_____
_____
_____
_____
_____
_____
_____
_____

✳ = Realizations   ★ = Ideas   # = To-do Items   Get Your Stuff Done!

I'm grateful for

1. _____

2. _____

3. _____

Today's Action Goals

Project: _____

☐ _____

☐ _____

☐ _____

Project: _____

☐ _____

☐ _____

☐ _____

Project: _____

☐ _____

☐ _____

☐ _____

Today's Wins

_____

_____

_____

Check-in

_____

_____

_____

Tomorrow, I will

_____

_____

_____

Date   State of Mind

_____

_____

_____

_____

_____

_____

_____

_____

_____

_____

_____

_____

_____

_____

_____

_____

_____

_____

_____

_____

_____

_____

_____

_____

_____

_____

_____

_____

_____

✳= Realizations   ★= Ideas   # = To-do Items   Get Your Stuff Done!

I'm grateful for

1. _____
2. _____
3. _____

Today's Action Goals

Project: _____

☐ _____
☐ _____
☐ _____

Project: _____

☐ _____
☐ _____
☐ _____

Project: _____

☐ _____
☐ _____
☐ _____

Today's Wins

_____
_____
_____

Check-in

_____
_____
_____

Tomorrow, I will

_____
_____
_____

Date State of Mind

✻ = Realizations   ★ = Ideas   # = To-do Items   Get Your Stuff Done!

I'm grateful for

1. _____

2. _____

3. _____

Today's Action Goals

Project: _____

☐ _____

☐ _____

☐ _____

Project: _____

☐ _____

☐ _____

☐ _____

Project: _____

☐ _____

☐ _____

☐ _____

Today's Wins

_____

_____

_____

Check-in

_____

_____

_____

Tomorrow, I will

_____

_____

_____

Date   State of Mind

_____

_____

_____

_____

_____

_____

_____

_____

_____

_____

_____

_____

_____

_____

_____

_____

_____

_____

_____

_____

_____

_____

_____

_____

_____

_____

_____

_____

_____

_____

✳ = Realizations   ★ = Ideas   # = To-do Items   Get Your Stuff Done!

I'm grateful for

1. _____
2. _____
3. _____

Today's Action Goals

Project: _____

☐ _____
☐ _____
☐ _____

Project: _____

☐ _____
☐ _____
☐ _____

Project: _____

☐ _____
☐ _____
☐ _____

Today's Wins

_____

_____

_____

Check-in

_____

_____

_____

Tomorrow, I will

_____

_____

_____

Date   State of Mind

*= Realizations   ★= Ideas # = To-do Items   Get Your Stuff Done!

I'm grateful for

1. _____
2. _____
3. _____

Today's Action Goals

Project: _____
- ☐ _____
- ☐ _____
- ☐ _____

Project: _____
- ☐ _____
- ☐ _____
- ☐ _____

Project: _____
- ☐ _____
- ☐ _____
- ☐ _____

Today's Wins

_____
_____
_____

Check-in

_____
_____
_____

Tomorrow, I will

_____
_____
_____

Date   State of Mind

I'm grateful for

1. _____
2. _____
3. _____

Today's Action Goals

Project: _____

☐ _____
☐ _____
☐ _____

Project: _____

☐ _____
☐ _____
☐ _____

Project: _____

☐ _____
☐ _____
☐ _____

Today's Wins

_____
_____
_____

Check-in

_____
_____
_____

Tomorrow, I will

_____
_____
_____

Weekly Assessment

Key Realizations

_____

_____

_____

_____

_____

Key Accomplishments

_____

_____

_____

_____

_____

Projects I Made Progress On

_____

_____

_____

_____

_____

Projects I Want To Work On

_____

_____

_____

_____

_____

✳ = Realizations   ★ = Ideas   # = To-do Items   Get Your Stuff Done!

Notes

_____

_____

_____

_____

_____

_____

_____

_____

_____

_____

_____

I Feel

_____

_____

_____

_____

_____

_____

_____

_____

_____

_____

Date   State of Mind

_____

_____

_____

_____

_____

_____

_____

_____

_____

_____

_____

_____

_____

_____

_____

_____

_____

_____

_____

_____

_____

_____

_____

_____

_____

_____

_____

_____

_____

_____

_____

_____

✳ = Realizations   ★ = Ideas   # = To-do Items   Get Your Stuff Done!

I'm grateful for

1. _____
2. _____
3. _____

Today's Action Goals

Project: _____

☐ _____
☐ _____
☐ _____

Project: _____

☐ _____
☐ _____
☐ _____

Project: _____

☐ _____
☐ _____
☐ _____

Today's Wins

_____
_____
_____

Check-in

_____
_____
_____

Tomorrow, I will

_____
_____
_____

Date   State of Mind

_____
_____
_____
_____
_____
_____
_____
_____
_____
_____
_____
_____
_____
_____
_____
_____
_____
_____
_____
_____
_____
_____
_____
_____
_____
_____
_____
_____
_____
_____

✳ = Realizations   ★ = Ideas   # = To-do Items   Get Your Stuff Done!

I'm grateful for

1. _____

2. _____

3. _____

Today's Action Goals

Project: _____

☐ _____

☐ _____

☐ _____

Project: _____

☐ _____

☐ _____

☐ _____

Project: _____

☐ _____

☐ _____

☐ _____

Today's Wins

_____

_____

_____

Check-in

_____

_____

_____

Tomorrow, I will

_____

_____

_____

Date   State of Mind

I'm grateful for

1. _____
2. _____
3. _____

Today's Action Goals

Project: _____

- ☐ _____
- ☐ _____
- ☐ _____

Project: _____

- ☐ _____
- ☐ _____
- ☐ _____

Project: _____

- ☐ _____
- ☐ _____
- ☐ _____

Today's Wins

_____

_____

_____

Check-in

_____

_____

_____

Tomorrow, I will

_____

_____

_____

Date State of Mind

_____
_____
_____
_____
_____
_____
_____
_____
_____
_____
_____
_____
_____
_____
_____
_____
_____
_____
_____
_____
_____
_____
_____
_____
_____
_____
_____
_____

✳ = Realizations ★ = Ideas # = To-do Items Get Your Stuff Done!

I'm grateful for

1. _____
2. _____
3. _____

Today's Action Goals

Project: _____
- ☐ _____
- ☐ _____
- ☐ _____

Project: _____
- ☐ _____
- ☐ _____
- ☐ _____

Project: _____
- ☐ _____
- ☐ _____
- ☐ _____

Today's Wins

_____

_____

_____

Check-in

_____

_____

_____

Tomorrow, I will

_____

_____

_____

Date   State of Mind

_____

_____

_____

_____

_____

_____

_____

_____

_____

_____

_____

_____

_____

_____

_____

_____

_____

_____

_____

_____

_____

_____

_____

_____

_____

_____

*= Realizations   ★= Ideas   # = To-do Items   Get Your Stuff Done!

I'm grateful for

1. _____
2. _____
3. _____

Today's Action Goals

Project: _____

☐ _____
☐ _____
☐ _____

Project: _____

☐ _____
☐ _____
☐ _____

Project: _____

☐ _____
☐ _____
☐ _____

Today's Wins

_____

_____

_____

Check-in

_____

_____

_____

Tomorrow, I will

_____

_____

_____

Date   State of Mind

_____

_____

_____

_____

_____

_____

_____

_____

_____

_____

_____

_____

_____

_____

_____

_____

_____

_____

_____

_____

_____

_____

_____

_____

_____

_____

_____

_____

_____

* = Realizations   ★ = Ideas   # = To-do Items   Get Your Stuff Done!

I'm grateful for

1. _____
2. _____
3. _____

Today's Action Goals

Project: _____

☐ _____
☐ _____
☐ _____

Project: _____

☐ _____
☐ _____
☐ _____

Project: _____

☐ _____
☐ _____
☐ _____

Today's Wins

_____
_____
_____

Check-in

_____
_____
_____

Tomorrow, I will

_____
_____
_____

Date   State of Mind

_____

_____

_____

_____

_____

_____

_____

_____

_____

_____

_____

_____

_____

_____

_____

_____

_____

_____

_____

_____

_____

_____

_____

_____

_____

_____

_____

_____

_____

_____

_____

✳ = Realizations   ★ = Ideas   # = To-do Items   Get Your Stuff Done!

I'm grateful for

1. _____
2. _____
3. _____

Today's Action Goals

Project: _____
- ☐ _____
- ☐ _____
- ☐ _____

Project: _____
- ☐ _____
- ☐ _____
- ☐ _____

Project: _____
- ☐ _____
- ☐ _____
- ☐ _____

Today's Wins

_____

_____

_____

Check-in

_____

_____

_____

Tomorrow, I will

_____

_____

_____

Date   State of Mind

Weekly Assessment

Key Realizations

_____

_____

_____

_____

_____

Key Accomplishments

_____

_____

_____

_____

Projects I Made Progress On

_____

_____

_____

_____

Projects I Want To Work On

_____

_____

_____

_____

_____

✳ = Realizations   ★ = Ideas   # = To-do Items   Get Your Stuff Done!

Notes

_____
_____
_____
_____
_____
_____
_____
_____
_____
_____
_____
_____

I Feel

_____
_____
_____
_____
_____
_____
_____
_____
_____
_____
_____
_____

Date   State of Mind

_____

_____

_____

_____

_____

_____

_____

_____

_____

_____

_____

_____

_____

_____

_____

_____

_____

_____

_____

_____

_____

_____

_____

_____

_____

_____

_____

_____

_____

* = Realizations   ★ = Ideas   # = To-do Items   Get Your Stuff Done!

I'm grateful for

1.

2.

3.

Today's Action Goals

Project:

☐

☐

☐

Project:

☐

☐

☐

Project:

☐

☐

☐

Today's Wins

Check-in

Tomorrow, I will

Date   State of Mind

_____

_____

_____

_____

_____

_____

_____

_____

_____

_____

_____

_____

_____

_____

_____

_____

_____

_____

_____

_____

_____

_____

_____

_____

_____

_____

_____

_____

_____

_____

_____

✳ = Realizations   ★ = Ideas # = To-do Items   Get Your Stuff Done!

I'm grateful for

1. _____
2. _____
3. _____

Today's Action Goals

Project: _____
- ☐ _____
- ☐ _____
- ☐ _____

Project: _____
- ☐ _____
- ☐ _____
- ☐ _____

Project: _____
- ☐ _____
- ☐ _____
- ☐ _____

Today's Wins

_____
_____
_____

Check-in

_____
_____
_____

Tomorrow, I will

_____
_____
_____

Date   State of Mind

* = Realizations   ★ = Ideas # = To-do Items   Get Your Stuff Done!

I'm grateful for

1. _____
2. _____
3. _____

Today's Action Goals

Project: _____

☐ _____
☐ _____
☐ _____

Project: _____

☐ _____
☐ _____
☐ _____

Project: _____

☐ _____
☐ _____
☐ _____

Today's Wins

_____

_____

_____

Check-in

_____

_____

_____

Tomorrow, I will

_____

_____

_____

Date   State of Mind

_____

_____

_____

_____

_____

_____

_____

_____

_____

_____

_____

_____

_____

_____

_____

_____

_____

_____

_____

_____

_____

_____

_____

_____

_____

_____

_____

_____

_____

_____

_____

✳= Realizations   ★= Ideas   # = To-do Items   Get Your Stuff Done!

I'm grateful for

1. _____
2. _____
3. _____

Today's Action Goals

Project: _____
- ☐ _____
- ☐ _____
- ☐ _____

Project: _____
- ☐ _____
- ☐ _____
- ☐ _____

Project: _____
- ☐ _____
- ☐ _____
- ☐ _____

Today's Wins

_____
_____
_____

Check-in

_____
_____
_____

Tomorrow, I will

_____
_____
_____

Date   State of Mind

_____

_____

_____

_____

_____

_____

_____

_____

_____

_____

_____

_____

_____

_____

_____

_____

_____

_____

_____

_____

_____

_____

_____

_____

_____

_____

_____

_____

_____

_____

✳ = Realizations   ★ = Ideas # = To-do Items   Get Your Stuff Done!

I'm grateful for

1. _____
2. _____
3. _____

Today's Action Goals

Project: _____

- ☐ _____
- ☐ _____
- ☐ _____

Project: _____

- ☐ _____
- ☐ _____
- ☐ _____

Project: _____

- ☐ _____
- ☐ _____
- ☐ _____

Today's Wins

_____

_____

_____

Check-in

_____

_____

_____

Tomorrow, I will

_____

_____

_____

Date   State of Mind

_____

_____

_____

_____

_____

_____

_____

_____

_____

_____

_____

_____

_____

_____

_____

_____

_____

_____

_____

_____

_____

_____

_____

_____

_____

_____

_____

_____

_____

✳ = Realizations   ★ = Ideas   # = To-do Items   Get Your Stuff Done!

I'm grateful for

1. _____
2. _____
3. _____

Today's Action Goals

Project: _____
- ☐ _____
- ☐ _____
- ☐ _____

Project: _____
- ☐ _____
- ☐ _____
- ☐ _____

Project: _____
- ☐ _____
- ☐ _____
- ☐ _____

Today's Wins

_____
_____
_____

Check-in

_____
_____
_____

Tomorrow, I will

_____
_____
_____

Date   State of Mind

I'm grateful for

1. _____

2. _____

3. _____

Today's Action Goals

Project: _____

☐ _____

☐ _____

☐ _____

Project: _____

☐ _____

☐ _____

☐ _____

Project: _____

☐ _____

☐ _____

☐ _____

Today's Wins

_____

_____

_____

Check-in

_____

_____

_____

Tomorrow, I will

_____

_____

_____

Weekly Assessment

Key Realizations

_____

_____

_____

_____

_____

Key Accomplishments

_____

_____

_____

_____

_____

Projects I Made Progress On

_____

_____

_____

_____

_____

Projects I Want To Work On

_____

_____

_____

_____

_____

Notes

_____

_____

_____

_____

_____

_____

_____

_____

_____

_____

_____

I Feel

_____

_____

_____

_____

_____

_____

_____

_____

_____

_____

_____

Date   State of Mind

_____
_____
_____
_____
_____
_____
_____
_____
_____
_____
_____
_____
_____
_____
_____
_____
_____
_____
_____
_____
_____
_____
_____
_____
_____
_____
_____
_____
_____
_____

✳ = Realizations   ★ = Ideas   # = To-do Items   Get Your Stuff Done!

I'm grateful for

1. _____
2. _____
3. _____

Today's Action Goals

Project: _____

☐ _____
☐ _____
☐ _____

Project: _____

☐ _____
☐ _____
☐ _____

Project: _____

☐ _____
☐ _____
☐ _____

Today's Wins

_____
_____
_____

Check-in

_____
_____
_____

Tomorrow, I will

_____
_____
_____

Date   State of Mind

*= Realizations ★= Ideas # = To-do Items Get Your Stuff Done!

I'm grateful for

1. _____

2. _____

3. _____

Today's Action Goals

Project: _____

☐ _____

☐ _____

☐ _____

Project: _____

☐ _____

☐ _____

☐ _____

Project: _____

☐ _____

☐ _____

☐ _____

Today's Wins

_____

_____

_____

Check-in

_____

_____

_____

Tomorrow, I will

_____

_____

_____

Date   State of Mind

_____

_____

_____

_____

_____

_____

_____

_____

_____

_____

_____

_____

_____

_____

_____

_____

_____

_____

_____

_____

_____

_____

_____

_____

_____

_____

_____

_____

_____

_____

_____

_____

✳ = Realizations   ★ = Ideas   # = To-do Items   Get Your Stuff Done!

I'm grateful for

1. _____
2. _____
3. _____

Today's Action Goals

Project: _____

☐ _____
☐ _____
☐ _____

Project: _____

☐ _____
☐ _____
☐ _____

Project: _____

☐ _____
☐ _____
☐ _____

Today's Wins

_____
_____
_____

Check-in

_____
_____
_____

Tomorrow, I will

_____
_____
_____

Date   State of Mind

_____

_____

_____

_____

_____

_____

_____

_____

_____

_____

_____

_____

_____

_____

_____

_____

_____

_____

_____

_____

_____

_____

_____

_____

_____

_____

_____

_____

_____

✳ = Realizations   ★ = Ideas   # = To-do Items   Get Your Stuff Done!

I'm grateful for

1. _____
2. _____
3. _____

Today's Action Goals

Project: _____

☐ _____
☐ _____
☐ _____

Project: _____

☐ _____
☐ _____
☐ _____

Project: _____

☐ _____
☐ _____
☐ _____

Today's Wins

_____
_____
_____

Check-in

_____
_____
_____

Tomorrow, I will

_____
_____
_____

Date   State of Mind

_____

_____

_____

_____

_____

_____

_____

_____

_____

_____

_____

_____

_____

_____

_____

_____

_____

_____

_____

_____

_____

_____

_____

_____

_____

_____

_____

_____

_____

_____

_____

✱ = Realizations   ★ = Ideas   # = To-do Items   Get Your Stuff Done!

I'm grateful for

1. _____
2. _____
3. _____

Today's Action Goals

Project: _____
- ☐ _____
- ☐ _____
- ☐ _____

Project: _____
- ☐ _____
- ☐ _____
- ☐ _____

Project: _____
- ☐ _____
- ☐ _____
- ☐ _____

Today's Wins

_____

_____

_____

Check-in

_____

_____

_____

Tomorrow, I will

_____

_____

_____

Date   State of Mind

_____

_____

_____

_____

_____

_____

_____

_____

_____

_____

_____

_____

_____

_____

_____

_____

_____

_____

_____

_____

_____

_____

_____

_____

_____

_____

_____

_____

_____

_____

_____

_____

_____

✳ = Realizations   ★ = Ideas   # = To-do Items   Get Your Stuff Done!

I'm grateful for

1. _____
2. _____
3. _____

Today's Action Goals

Project: _____
- ☐ _____
- ☐ _____
- ☐ _____

Project: _____
- ☐ _____
- ☐ _____
- ☐ _____

Project: _____
- ☐ _____
- ☐ _____
- ☐ _____

Today's Wins

_____

_____

_____

Check-in

_____

_____

_____

Tomorrow, I will

_____

_____

_____

Date   State of Mind

_____
_____
_____
_____
_____
_____
_____
_____
_____
_____
_____
_____
_____
_____
_____
_____
_____
_____
_____
_____
_____
_____
_____
_____
_____
_____
_____
_____
_____
_____

✻ = Realizations   ★ = Ideas   # = To-do Items   Get Your Stuff Done!

I'm grateful for

1. _____

2. _____

3. _____

Today's Action Goals

Project: _____

☐ _____

☐ _____

☐ _____

Project: _____

☐ _____

☐ _____

☐ _____

Project: _____

☐ _____

☐ _____

☐ _____

Today's Wins

_____

_____

_____

Check-in

_____

_____

_____

Tomorrow, I will

_____

_____

_____

Date   State of Mind

Weekly Assessment

Key Realizations

_____

_____

_____

_____

_____

Key Accomplishments

_____

_____

_____

_____

_____

Projects I Made Progress On

_____

_____

_____

_____

_____

Projects I Want To Work On

_____

_____

_____

_____

_____

＊= Realizations   ★= Ideas # = To-do Items   Get Your Stuff Done!

Notes

_____

_____

_____

_____

_____

_____

_____

_____

_____

_____

_____

_____

I Feel

_____

_____

_____

_____

_____

_____

_____

_____

_____

_____

Date   State of Mind

I'm grateful for

1. _____
2. _____
3. _____

Today's Action Goals

Project: _____

☐ _____
☐ _____
☐ _____

Project: _____

☐ _____
☐ _____
☐ _____

Project: _____

☐ _____
☐ _____
☐ _____

Today's Wins

_____
_____
_____

Check-in

_____
_____
_____

Tomorrow, I will

_____
_____
_____

Date State of Mind

＊= Realizations　★= Ideas　# = To-do Items　Get Your Stuff Done!

I'm grateful for

1. _____
2. _____
3. _____

Today's Action Goals

Project: _____
- ☐ _____
- ☐ _____
- ☐ _____

Project: _____
- ☐ _____
- ☐ _____
- ☐ _____

Project: _____
- ☐ _____
- ☐ _____
- ☐ _____

Today's Wins

_____

_____

_____

Check-in

_____

_____

_____

Tomorrow, I will

_____

_____

_____

Date   State of Mind

_____

_____

_____

_____

_____

_____

_____

_____

_____

_____

_____

_____

_____

_____

_____

_____

_____

_____

_____

_____

_____

_____

_____

_____

_____

_____

_____

_____

✳ = Realizations   ★ = Ideas   # = To-do Items   Get Your Stuff Done!

I'm grateful for

1. _____
2. _____
3. _____

Today's Action Goals

Project: _____

- ☐ _____
- ☐ _____
- ☐ _____

Project: _____

- ☐ _____
- ☐ _____
- ☐ _____

Project: _____

- ☐ _____
- ☐ _____
- ☐ _____

Today's Wins

_____

_____

Check-in

_____

_____

Tomorrow, I will

_____

_____

_____

Date   State of Mind

_____
_____
_____
_____
_____
_____
_____
_____
_____
_____
_____
_____
_____
_____
_____
_____
_____
_____
_____
_____
_____
_____
_____
_____
_____
_____
_____
_____
_____

✳ = Realizations   ★ = Ideas   # = To-do Items   Get Your Stuff Done!

I'm grateful for

1. _____
2. _____
3. _____

Today's Action Goals

Project: _____

☐ _____
☐ _____
☐ _____

Project: _____

☐ _____
☐ _____
☐ _____

Project: _____

☐ _____
☐ _____
☐ _____

Today's Wins

_____
_____
_____

Check-in

_____
_____
_____

Tomorrow, I will

_____
_____
_____

Date   State of Mind

---

* = Realizations   ★ = Ideas   # = To-do Items   Get Your Stuff Done!

I'm grateful for

1. _____
2. _____
3. _____

Today's Action Goals

Project: _____

☐ _____
☐ _____
☐ _____

Project: _____

☐ _____
☐ _____
☐ _____

Project: _____

☐ _____
☐ _____
☐ _____

Today's Wins

_____

_____

_____

Check-in

_____

_____

_____

Tomorrow, I will

_____

_____

_____

Date   State of Mind

_____

_____

_____

_____

_____

_____

_____

_____

_____

_____

_____

_____

_____

_____

_____

_____

_____

_____

_____

_____

_____

_____

_____

_____

_____

_____

_____

_____

_____

_____

_____

_____

*= Realizations   ★= Ideas   # = To-do Items   Get Your Stuff Done!

I'm grateful for

1. _____
2. _____
3. _____

Today's Action Goals

Project: _____
- [ ] _____
- [ ] _____
- [ ] _____

Project: _____
- [ ] _____
- [ ] _____
- [ ] _____

Project: _____
- [ ] _____
- [ ] _____
- [ ] _____

Today's Wins

_____

_____

_____

Check-in

_____

_____

_____

Tomorrow, I will

_____

_____

_____

Date   State of Mind

✴ = Realizations   ★ = Ideas # = To-do Items   Get Your Stuff Done!

I'm grateful for

1.
2.
3.

Today's Action Goals

Project:
☐
☐
☐

Project:
☐
☐
☐

Project:
☐
☐
☐

Today's Wins

Check-in

Tomorrow, I will

Date   State of Mind

Weekly Assessment

Key Realizations

_____

_____

_____

_____

_____

Key Accomplishments

_____

_____

_____

_____

Projects I Made Progress On

_____

_____

_____

_____

Projects I Want To Work On

_____

_____

_____

_____

✳= Realizations   ★= Ideas   # = To-do Items   Get Your Stuff Done!

Notes

_____

_____

_____

_____

_____

_____

_____

_____

_____

_____

I Feel

_____

_____

_____

_____

_____

_____

_____

_____

_____

_____

_____

Date   State of Mind

_____
_____
_____
_____
_____
_____
_____
_____
_____
_____
_____
_____
_____
_____
_____
_____
_____
_____
_____
_____
_____
_____
_____
_____
_____
_____
_____
_____
_____
_____

✳ = Realizations   ★ = Ideas   # = To-do Items   Get Your Stuff Done!

I'm grateful for

1. _____
2. _____
3. _____

Today's Action Goals

Project: _____

- ☐ _____
- ☐ _____
- ☐ _____

Project: _____

- ☐ _____
- ☐ _____
- ☐ _____

Project: _____

- ☐ _____
- ☐ _____
- ☐ _____

Today's Wins

_____

_____

_____

Check-in

_____

_____

_____

Tomorrow, I will

_____

_____

_____

Date   State of Mind

_____

_____

_____

_____

_____

_____

_____

_____

_____

_____

_____

_____

_____

_____

_____

_____

_____

_____

_____

_____

_____

_____

_____

_____

_____

_____

_____

_____

✳ = Realizations   **★** = Ideas # = To-do Items   Get Your Stuff Done!

I'm grateful for

1. _____

2. _____

3. _____

Today's Action Goals

Project: _____

☐ _____

☐ _____

☐ _____

Project: _____

☐ _____

☐ _____

☐ _____

Project: _____

☐ _____

☐ _____

☐ _____

Today's Wins

_____

_____

_____

Check-in

_____

_____

_____

Tomorrow, I will

_____

_____

_____

Date   State of Mind

_____
_____
_____
_____
_____
_____
_____
_____
_____
_____
_____
_____
_____
_____
_____
_____
_____
_____
_____
_____
_____
_____
_____
_____
_____
_____
_____
_____
_____
_____
_____
_____
_____

✳ = Realizations   ★ = Ideas   # = To-do Items   Get Your Stuff Done!

I'm grateful for

1. _____
2. _____
3. _____

Today's Action Goals

Project: _____
- ☐ _____
- ☐ _____
- ☐ _____

Project: _____
- ☐ _____
- ☐ _____
- ☐ _____

Project: _____
- ☐ _____
- ☐ _____
- ☐ _____

Today's Wins

_____

_____

_____

Check-in

_____

_____

_____

Tomorrow, I will

_____

_____

_____

Date   State of Mind

I'm grateful for

1. _____
2. _____
3. _____

Today's Action Goals

Project: _____
- ☐ _____
- ☐ _____
- ☐ _____

Project: _____
- ☐ _____
- ☐ _____
- ☐ _____

Project: _____
- ☐ _____
- ☐ _____
- ☐ _____

Today's Wins

_____

_____

_____

Check-in

_____

_____

_____

Tomorrow, I will

_____

_____

_____

Date   State of Mind

_____

_____

_____

_____

_____

_____

_____

_____

_____

_____

_____

_____

_____

_____

_____

_____

_____

_____

_____

_____

_____

_____

_____

_____

_____

_____

_____

_____

_____

_____

_____

* = Realizations   ★ = Ideas   # = To-do Items   Get Your Stuff Done!

I'm grateful for

1. _____
2. _____
3. _____

Today's Action Goals

Project: _____

☐ _____
☐ _____
☐ _____

Project: _____

☐ _____
☐ _____
☐ _____

Project: _____

☐ _____
☐ _____
☐ _____

Today's Wins

_____
_____
_____

Check-in

_____
_____
_____

Tomorrow, I will

_____
_____
_____

Date   State of Mind

_____

I'm grateful for

1. _____
2. _____
3. _____

Today's Action Goals

Project: _____

- ☐ _____
- ☐ _____
- ☐ _____

Project: _____

- ☐ _____
- ☐ _____
- ☐ _____

Project: _____

- ☐ _____
- ☐ _____
- ☐ _____

Today's Wins

_____

_____

_____

Check-in

_____

_____

_____

Tomorrow, I will

_____

_____

_____

Date   State of Mind

_____

_____

_____

_____

_____

_____

_____

_____

_____

_____

_____

_____

_____

_____

_____

_____

_____

_____

_____

_____

_____

_____

_____

_____

_____

_____

_____

_____

* = Realizations   ★ = Ideas   # = To-do Items   Get Your Stuff Done!

I'm grateful for

1. _____

2. _____

3. _____

Today's Action Goals

Project: _____

☐ _____

☐ _____

☐ _____

Project: _____

☐ _____

☐ _____

☐ _____

Project: _____

☐ _____

☐ _____

☐ _____

Today's Wins

_____

_____

_____

Check-in

_____

_____

_____

Tomorrow, I will

_____

_____

_____

Date   State of Mind

Weekly Assessment

Key Realizations

_____

_____

_____

_____

_____

Key Accomplishments

_____

_____

_____

_____

_____

Projects I Made Progress On

_____

_____

_____

_____

_____

Projects I Want To Work On

_____

_____

_____

_____

_____

✱= Realizations   ★= Ideas   # = To-do Items   Get Your Stuff Done!

End of the Day Goals, Wins, and Intentions

Notes

_____

_____

_____

_____

_____

_____

_____

_____

_____

_____

I Feel

_____

_____

_____

_____

_____

_____

_____

_____

_____

_____

Date   State of Mind

_____
_____
_____
_____
_____
_____
_____
_____
_____
_____
_____
_____
_____
_____
_____
_____
_____
_____
_____
_____
_____
_____
_____
_____
_____
_____
_____
_____
_____
_____

✳ = Realizations   ★ = Ideas   # = To-do Items   Get Your Stuff Done!

I'm grateful for

1. _____
2. _____
3. _____

Today's Action Goals

Project: _____
- ☐ _____
- ☐ _____
- ☐ _____

Project: _____
- ☐ _____
- ☐ _____
- ☐ _____

Project: _____
- ☐ _____
- ☐ _____
- ☐ _____

Today's Wins

_____
_____
_____

Check-in

_____
_____
_____

Tomorrow, I will

_____
_____
_____

Date   State of Mind

_____

_____

_____

_____

_____

_____

_____

_____

_____

_____

_____

_____

_____

_____

_____

_____

_____

_____

_____

_____

_____

_____

_____

_____

_____

_____

_____

_____

_____

✳ = Realizations   ★ = Ideas   # = To-do Items   Get Your Stuff Done!

I'm grateful for

1. _____

2. _____

3. _____

Today's Action Goals

Project: _____

☐ _____

☐ _____

☐ _____

Project: _____

☐ _____

☐ _____

☐ _____

Project: _____

☐ _____

☐ _____

☐ _____

Today's Wins

_____

_____

_____

Check-in

_____

_____

_____

Tomorrow, I will

_____

_____

_____

Date   State of Mind

＊= Realizations   ★= Ideas # = To-do Items Get Your Stuff Done!

I'm grateful for

1. _____
2. _____
3. _____

Today's Action Goals

Project: _____

☐ _____
☐ _____
☐ _____

Project: _____

☐ _____
☐ _____
☐ _____

Project: _____

☐ _____
☐ _____
☐ _____

Today's Wins

_____

_____

_____

Check-in

_____

_____

_____

Tomorrow, I will

_____

_____

_____

Date   State of Mind

_____
_____
_____
_____
_____
_____
_____
_____
_____
_____
_____
_____
_____
_____
_____
_____
_____
_____
_____
_____
_____
_____
_____
_____
_____
_____
_____
_____
_____
_____
_____
_____

✱ = Realizations   ★ = Ideas   # = To-do Items   Get Your Stuff Done!

I'm grateful for

1.
2.
3.

Today's Action Goals

Project:
- ☐
- ☐
- ☐

Project:
- ☐
- ☐
- ☐

Project:
- ☐
- ☐
- ☐

Today's Wins

Check-in

Tomorrow, I will

Date State of Mind

I'm grateful for

1. _____

2. _____

3. _____

Today's Action Goals

Project: _____

☐ _____

☐ _____

☐ _____

Project: _____

☐ _____

☐ _____

☐ _____

Project: _____

☐ _____

☐ _____

☐ _____

Today's Wins

_____

_____

_____

Check-in

_____

_____

_____

Tomorrow, I will

_____

_____

_____

Date   State of Mind

_____

_____

_____

_____

_____

_____

_____

_____

_____

_____

_____

_____

_____

_____

_____

_____

_____

_____

_____

_____

_____

_____

_____

_____

_____

_____

_____

_____

_____

_____

_____

_____

_____

_____

*= Realizations   ★= Ideas   # = To-do Items   Get Your Stuff Done!

I'm grateful for

1. _____
2. _____
3. _____

Today's Action Goals

Project: _____

☐ _____
☐ _____
☐ _____

Project: _____

☐ _____
☐ _____
☐ _____

Project: _____

☐ _____
☐ _____
☐ _____

Today's Wins

_____

_____

_____

Check-in

_____

_____

_____

Tomorrow, I will

_____

_____

_____

Date   State of Mind

_____

_____

_____

_____

_____

_____

_____

_____

_____

_____

_____

_____

_____

_____

_____

_____

_____

_____

_____

_____

_____

_____

_____

_____

_____

_____

_____

_____

_____

✳ = Realizations   ★ = Ideas   # = To-do Items   Get Your Stuff Done!

I'm grateful for

1. _____
2. _____
3. _____

Today's Action Goals

Project: _____

☐ _____
☐ _____
☐ _____

Project: _____

☐ _____
☐ _____
☐ _____

Project: _____

☐ _____
☐ _____
☐ _____

Today's Wins

_____

_____

_____

Check-in

_____

_____

_____

Tomorrow, I will

_____

_____

_____

Weekly Assessment

Key Realizations

_____

_____

_____

_____

_____

Key Accomplishments

_____

_____

_____

_____

_____

Projects I Made Progress On

_____

_____

_____

_____

_____

Projects I Want To Work On

_____

_____

_____

_____

_____

＊= Realizations   ★= Ideas   # = To-do Items   Get Your Stuff Done!

Notes

_____

_____

_____

_____

_____

_____

_____

_____

_____

_____

_____

I Feel

_____

_____

_____

_____

_____

_____

_____

_____

_____

_____

_____

_____

Date   State of Mind

_____

_____

_____

_____

_____

_____

_____

_____

_____

_____

_____

_____

_____

_____

_____

_____

_____

_____

_____

_____

_____

_____

_____

_____

_____

_____

_____

_____

_____

✳ = Realizations   ★ = Ideas   # = To-do Items   Get Your Stuff Done!

I'm grateful for

1. _____

2. _____

3. _____

Today's Action Goals

Project: _____

☐ _____

☐ _____

☐ _____

Project: _____

☐ _____

☐ _____

☐ _____

Project: _____

☐ _____

☐ _____

☐ _____

Today's Wins

_____

_____

_____

Check-in

_____

_____

_____

Tomorrow, I will

_____

_____

_____

Date   State of Mind

＊= Realizations   ★= Ideas   # = To-do Items   Get Your Stuff Done!

I'm grateful for

1. _____
2. _____
3. _____

Today's Action Goals

Project: _____
- ☐ _____
- ☐ _____
- ☐ _____

Project: _____
- ☐ _____
- ☐ _____
- ☐ _____

Project: _____
- ☐ _____
- ☐ _____
- ☐ _____

Today's Wins

_____

_____

_____

Check-in

_____

_____

_____

Tomorrow, I will

_____

_____

_____

Date   State of Mind

*= Realizations   ★= Ideas # = To-do Items   Get Your Stuff Done!

I'm grateful for

1. _____
2. _____
3. _____

Today's Action Goals

Project: _____
☐ _____
☐ _____
☐ _____

Project: _____
☐ _____
☐ _____
☐ _____

Project: _____
☐ _____
☐ _____
☐ _____

Today's Wins

_____

_____

_____

Check-in

_____

_____

_____

Tomorrow, I will

_____

_____

_____

Date   State of Mind

* = Realizations   **★** = Ideas   # = To-do Items   Get Your Stuff Done!

I'm grateful for

1. _____
2. _____
3. _____

Today's Action Goals

Project: _____

☐ _____
☐ _____
☐ _____

Project: _____

☐ _____
☐ _____
☐ _____

Project: _____

☐ _____
☐ _____
☐ _____

Today's Wins

_____

_____

_____

Check-in

_____

_____

_____

Tomorrow, I will

_____

_____

_____

Date   State of Mind

*＝ Realizations   ★＝ Ideas # ＝ To-do Items   Get Your Stuff Done!

I'm grateful for

1. _____

2. _____

3. _____

Today's Action Goals

Project: _____

☐ _____

☐ _____

☐ _____

Project: _____

☐ _____

☐ _____

☐ _____

Project: _____

☐ _____

☐ _____

☐ _____

Today's Wins

_____

_____

_____

Check-in

_____

_____

_____

Tomorrow, I will

_____

_____

_____

Date   State of Mind

I'm grateful for

1. _____

2. _____

3. _____

Today's Action Goals

Project: _____

☐ _____

☐ _____

☐ _____

Project: _____

☐ _____

☐ _____

☐ _____

Project: _____

☐ _____

☐ _____

☐ _____

Today's Wins

_____

_____

_____

Check-in

_____

_____

_____

Tomorrow, I will

_____

_____

_____

Date   State of Mind

*= Realizations   ★= Ideas   # = To-do Items   Get Your Stuff Done!

I'm grateful for

1. _____
2. _____
3. _____

Today's Action Goals

Project: _____

☐ _____
☐ _____
☐ _____

Project: _____

☐ _____
☐ _____
☐ _____

Project: _____

☐ _____
☐ _____
☐ _____

Today's Wins

_____
_____
_____

Check-in

_____
_____
_____

Tomorrow, I will

_____
_____
_____

Date   State of Mind

Weekly Assessment

Key Realizations

_____

_____

_____

_____

_____

Key Accomplishments

_____

_____

_____

_____

_____

Projects I Made Progress On

_____

_____

_____

_____

Projects I Want To Work On

_____

_____

_____

_____

* = Realizations   ★ = Ideas # = To-do Items Get Your Stuff Done!

Notes

_____

_____

_____

_____

_____

_____

_____

_____

_____

_____

_____

_____

I Feel

_____

_____

_____

_____

_____

_____

_____

_____

_____

_____

_____

Date   State of Mind

*= Realizations   ★= Ideas # = To-do Items Get Your Stuff Done!

I'm grateful for

1. _____

2. _____

3. _____

Today's Action Goals

Project: _____

☐ _____

☐ _____

☐ _____

Project: _____

☐ _____

☐ _____

☐ _____

Project: _____

☐ _____

☐ _____

☐ _____

Today's Wins

_____

_____

_____

Check-in

_____

_____

_____

Tomorrow, I will

_____

_____

_____

Date   State of Mind

_____

_____

_____

_____

_____

_____

_____

_____

_____

_____

_____

_____

_____

_____

_____

_____

_____

_____

_____

_____

_____

_____

_____

_____

_____

_____

*= Realizations   ★= Ideas   # = To-do Items   Get Your Stuff Done!

I'm grateful for

1. _____
2. _____
3. _____

Today's Action Goals

Project: _____

☐ _____

☐ _____

☐ _____

Project: _____

☐ _____

☐ _____

☐ _____

Project: _____

☐ _____

☐ _____

☐ _____

Today's Wins

_____

_____

_____

Check-in

_____

_____

_____

Tomorrow, I will

_____

_____

_____

Date   State of Mind

_____

_____

_____

_____

_____

_____

_____

_____

_____

_____

_____

_____

_____

_____

_____

_____

_____

_____

_____

_____

_____

_____

_____

_____

_____

_____

_____

_____

_____

_____

* = Realizations   ★ = Ideas   # = To-do Items   Get Your Stuff Done!

I'm grateful for

1. _____

2. _____

3. _____

Today's Action Goals

Project: _____

☐ _____

☐ _____

☐ _____

Project: _____

☐ _____

☐ _____

☐ _____

Project: _____

☐ _____

☐ _____

☐ _____

Today's Wins

_____

_____

_____

Check-in

_____

_____

_____

Tomorrow, I will

_____

_____

_____

Date State of Mind

*= Realizations ★= Ideas # = To-do Items Get Your Stuff Done!

I'm grateful for

1. _____
2. _____
3. _____

Today's Action Goals

Project: _____

☐ _____
☐ _____
☐ _____

Project: _____

☐ _____
☐ _____
☐ _____

Project: _____

☐ _____
☐ _____
☐ _____

Today's Wins

_____
_____
_____

Check-in

_____
_____
_____

Tomorrow, I will

_____
_____
_____

Date   State of Mind

✳ = Realizations   ★ = Ideas   # = To-do Items   Get Your Stuff Done!

I'm grateful for

1. _____
2. _____
3. _____

Today's Action Goals

Project: _____
- ☐ _____
- ☐ _____
- ☐ _____

Project: _____
- ☐ _____
- ☐ _____
- ☐ _____

Project: _____
- ☐ _____
- ☐ _____
- ☐ _____

Today's Wins

_____
_____
_____

Check-in

_____
_____
_____

Tomorrow, I will

_____
_____
_____

Date   State of Mind

✳ = Realizations   ★ = Ideas   # = To-do Items   Get Your Stuff Done!

I'm grateful for

1. _____

2. _____

3. _____

Today's Action Goals

Project: _____

☐ _____

☐ _____

☐ _____

Project: _____

☐ _____

☐ _____

☐ _____

Project: _____

☐ _____

☐ _____

☐ _____

Today's Wins

_____

_____

_____

Check-in

_____

_____

_____

Tomorrow, I will

_____

_____

_____

Date   State of Mind

_____
_____
_____
_____
_____
_____
_____
_____
_____
_____
_____
_____
_____
_____
_____
_____
_____
_____
_____
_____
_____
_____
_____
_____
_____

✷ = Realizations ★ = Ideas # = To-do Items Get Your Stuff Done!

I'm grateful for

1. _____
2. _____
3. _____

Today's Action Goals

Project: _____
☐ _____
☐ _____
☐ _____

Project: _____
☐ _____
☐ _____
☐ _____

Project: _____
☐ _____
☐ _____
☐ _____

Today's Wins

_____

_____

_____

Check-in

_____

_____

_____

Tomorrow, I will

_____

_____

_____

Date   State of Mind

Weekly Assessment

Key Realizations

_____

_____

_____

_____

_____

Key Accomplishments

_____

_____

_____

_____

_____

Projects I Made Progress On

_____

_____

_____

_____

_____

Projects I Want To Work On

_____

_____

_____

_____

_____

✳ = Realizations   ★ = Ideas   # = To-do Items   Get Your Stuff Done!

Notes

_____
_____
_____
_____
_____
_____
_____
_____
_____
_____
_____
_____

I Feel

_____
_____
_____
_____
_____
_____
_____
_____
_____
_____
_____
_____
_____

You Did It!

Self-Assessment (*How do I feel about what I've achieved?*)

_____

_____

_____

_____

_____

_____

_____

_____

_____

_____

Focus (*What do I want to focus on for the next 12 weeks?*)

_____

_____

_____

_____

_____

_____

_____

_____

_____

_____

✳ = Realizations   ★ = Ideas   # = To-do Items   Get Your Stuff Done!

NOW THAT YOU'VE FINISHED!

Congratulations! You've finished the journal! I hope you're super proud of what you've accomplished.

Do you remember the reward you wanted three months ago? If you still want it, **go reward yourself**. If not, choose another reward. Your desires might have changed as you achieved all these goals so it's cool if you want to modify it.

Regardless, go reward yourself. And then keep the principles in the journal going.

If you're enterprising, download the PDF of the journal (https://izoldat.com/gysd/). I recommend you print it double-sided on three-hole-punch paper. Then, put it in a three-ring binder and use it to achieve your goals.

Or, you can make things easier on yourself and get another copy of the journal on amazon.com (Find the link at https://izoldat.com/gysd/.)

Modify this practice to suit your unique architecture. Use the best of it. Lose the rest of it. But keep going! The goal here is to help you be more productive. Then, you'll have time for more juicy creativity in your life. You do this one step at a time. But each step will eventually help you climb mountains!

Contact me with any questions.

With love,

Izolda

ABOUT THE AUTHOR

Born in the former Soviet Union, Izolda conquered language barriers and became a heart-centered, engaging coach. As part of the year-long immigration process, she and her family lived in a war zone. During that time, she developed her strategies to manage stress and achieve goals. She traveled internationally as a Master Trainer for NASA. Today, she coaches her clients to develop their life systems. These individualized systems enable them to live productive, fulfilling, and joyful lives. She presents leadership, communication, and creativity programs all over the world. She lives in Brooklyn, NY with her husband and two cats. Izolda holds a BA in English from the University of Michigan. She loves to travel. She has a mission to visit one new country every year and meet as many new people as possible.

Connect with Izolda
Speaking and Programming: https://IzoldaT.com
Author Website: https://author.IzoldaT.com
Podcast: The Creative Mindset

Books by Izolda
Non-fiction
- Life Elements: Transform Your Life with Earth, Air, Fire, and Water
- Win the Day
- Speak From Within

Fiction
- The Fiddler's Talisman, Book One of the Fairy Godmother Diaries
- The Piano's Key, Book Two of the Fairy Godmother Diaries

Made in the USA
Middletown, DE
09 January 2020